SCHOLASTIC

Reading Response for Nonfiction
Graphic Organizers & Mini-Lessons

GRADES 2–4

JENNIFER JACOBSON

New York • Toronto • London • Auckland • Sydney
Mexico City • New Delhi • Hong Kong • Buenos Aires

Teaching *Resources*

Acknowledgments

Many thanks to Jim Becker, Danielle Blood, Kathleen Hollenbeck, and Mackie Rhodes

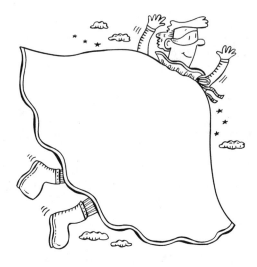

Teachers who wish to contact Jennifer about her staff development programs
may visit her Web site at www.jenniferjacobson.com.

Edited by Kathleen Hollenbeck
Cover design by Maria Lilja
Interior design by Holly Grundon
Interior illustrations by Teresa Anderko

ISBN-13: 978-0-439-57295-8
ISBN-10: 0-439-57295-9

Contents

Mini-Lessons

Introduction

Welcome to *Reading Response for Nonfiction: Graphic Organizers & Mini-Lessons*! Designed for flexible use, these 20 graphic organizers promote reading response, guide students to think about and analyze what they read, and lead them to read with deeper engagement.

Why Use Graphic Organizers for Reading Response?

Graphic organizers provide schemata: a way of structuring information or arranging key concepts into a pattern, enhancing comprehension and imparting useful learning strategies (Bromley et al., 1995). Organizers offer students an efficient way to direct their attention, record key information, display their thinking, and monitor their use of learning strategies.

Research has shown that graphic organizers help students to:

* connect prior knowledge to new information (Guastello, 2000).

* integrate language and thinking in an organized format (Bromley et al, 1995).

* increase comprehension and retention of text (Boyle & Weishaar, 1997; Chang et al., 2002; Moore & Readence, 1984).

* engage in mid- to high-level thinking along Bloom's Taxonomy (knowledge, comprehension, synthesis, and evaluation) (Dodge, 2005).

Why Ask Students to Respond to Nonfiction?

A major shift in reading expectations and content occurs around the third or fourth grade. Student focus shifts from "learning to read" to "reading to learn" (Chall, 1983). Hence, the importance and incidence of nonfiction reading rises sharply. That's why it's so important to take the time now to help students learn to navigate, interpret, and utilize nonfiction effectively.

Informational books expose students to concepts and specialized vocabulary, building background knowledge and language that they can draw upon when reading and discussing more complex books later (Yopp & Yopp, 2000). Additionally, students who reported reading a greater variety of texts—including informational texts—performed better on the National Assessment of Educational Progress (NAEP) (Dreher, 2003).

About Web Sites

Throughout this book you'll find Web site suggestions to support various activities. Please keep in mind that Internet locations and content can change over time. Always check Web sites in advance to make certain the intended information is still available.

How to Use This Book

The organizers in this book can be used in any order and lend themselves well to many forms of teaching: pre- and post-assessment, preparation for literature circles, and mini-lessons. They are suitable for use with the whole class, small groups, or individual students, and are ideal for homework or guided cooperative learning groups.

Each organizer targets a different skill or combination of skills, which is shown on each lesson page. At the top of the page, a purpose states the uses and benefits of the activity, and the suggestion for introducing the lesson helps set the stage and pique student interest. Step-by-step directions provide a guide for demonstrating how to use and complete the organizer. Also included is a helpful management tip, which recommends one or more specific ways to use the graphic organizer, and an activity that lets you take students a step further by building on the skills and strategies covered in the lesson or by using the organizer for a different purpose. Finally, to help you get started, the books and resources that are referred to in the sample lesson—or that might be appropriate for that particular lesson—are listed in the literature link on the page.

Using a Graphic Organizer

Select the graphic organizer that best suits your instructional needs. Then follow these suggestions to prepare and use the organizer with students.

* **Test It.** Before using an organizer, give it a "trial run" on your own to experience the process firsthand. This will allow you to see how well the graphic works with the selected text. Make any modifications necessary to best meet the needs of your students (Egan, 1999).

* **Present It.** Determine the best method for presenting the graphic organizer. You might make a photocopy for use as a transparency on the overhead projector, or distribute paper copies to students to complete as you model its use. Keep a supply of frequently used organizers on hand for students to use independently.

* **Model It.** Research has shown that graphic organizers are most effective when the teacher presents and models the organizer first for the whole group (Bowman et al., 1998). To ensure greatest success, model the use of each organizer with the whole class before asking students to complete it independently.

Helpful Hints for Success

* Introduce the graphic organizer *before* students read. That way, students will read with a strong sense of purpose and focus.

* Model the use of the organizer so that students will gain a clear understanding of its purpose and how to complete it.

* When analyzing text during a mini-lesson, think out loud. This will allow students to recognize and apply your strategies for greater reading comprehension.

* Provide adhesive note strips for students to mark passages that they will later refer to when completing their organizers.

* Urge students not to feel limited by the design of a graphic organizer. Demonstrate writing outside the lines and adding other shapes and lines when making new connections.

* Provide a rich selection of reading materials and a variety of reading response graphic organizers to use with them. This will help keep your reading program fresh and interesting.

> As teachers model their own response to literature (through thinking aloud and use of graphic organizers), they make reading strategies explicit. Regular modeling, opportunities to practice and apply the strategies, and consistency in contexts allow students to transfer this knowledge to independent reading and assessment situations (Pardo, 2004).

Assessing Student Performance

Graphic organizers allow you to assess a student's comprehension at a glance. You can use the organizers in this book to determine what students know, the depth of their understanding, what they need to know, what they retain after reading, and the connections they have made. For example, after students read a biography, you can have them complete Famous Footsteps (page 14) to assess their comprehension of the facts, experiences, and impact of that person's life.

Students can also use graphic organizers to assess their own learning. For example, after reading a nonfiction text about an animal or famous landmark, students can complete What's the Scoop? (page 34) to assess whether their prior knowledge aligns with facts presented in the piece, summarize their new knowledge, and determine what additional information they would like to learn.

Graphic organizers are a performance-based model of assessment and are ideal for including in student portfolios, as they require students to demonstrate both their grasp of the concept and their reasoning.

Connections to the Standards

This book is designed to support you in meeting the following reading standards outlined by Mid-continent Research for Education and Learning (McREL), an organization that collects and synthesizes national and state standards.

Uses the general skills and strategies of the reading process.

* Previews text (e.g. skims materials, uses pictures, textual clues, and text format).
* Establishes a purpose for reading (for information, for pleasure, to understand a specific viewpoint).
* Understands level-appropriate reading vocabulary (synonyms, antonyms, homophones, multi-meaning words).
* Monitors own reading strategies and makes modifications as needed (recognizes when he or she is confused by a section of text, questions whether the text makes sense).

Uses reading skills and strategies to understand and interpret a variety of literary texts.

* Uses reading skills and strategies to understand a variety of literary passages and texts (fairy tales, folktales, fiction, nonfiction, myths, poems, fables, fantasies, historical fiction, biographies, autobiographies, chapter books).
* Understands similarities and differences within and among literary works from various genres and cultures (in terms of settings, character types, events, points of view, role of natural phenomena).

Uses reading skills and strategies to understand and interpret a variety of informational texts.

* Uses reading skills and strategies to understand a variety of informational texts (textbooks, biographical sketches, letters, diaries, directions, procedures, magazines).
* Uses text organizers (headings, topic and summary sentences, graphic features, typeface, chapter titles) to determine the main idea and locate information.
* Uses the various parts of a book (index, table of contents, glossary, appendix, preface) to locate information.
* Summarizes and paraphrases information in texts (includes the main idea and significant supporting details of a reading selection).
* Uses prior knowledge and experience to understand and respond to new information.
* Understands structural patterns or organization in informational texts (chronological, logical, or sequential order; compare-and-contrast; cause-and-effect; proposition and support).

Kendall, J. S. & Marzano, R. J. (2004). *Content knowledge: A compendium of standards and benchmarks for K-12 education.* Aurora, CO: Mid-continent Research for Education and Learning. Online database: http://www.mcrel.org/standards-benchmarks/

References and Additional Resources

Bell, K. & Caspari, A. (May 2002). "Strategies for improving nonfiction reading comprehension." An Action Research Project; Saint Xavier University & Skylight Professional Development. Chicago, IL.

Bowman, L. A., Carpenter, J. & Paone, R. (1998). "Using graphic organizers, cooperative learning groups, and higher order thinking skills to improve reading comprehension." M.A. Action Research Project, Saint Xavier University. Chicago, IL.

Boyle, J. R. & Weishaar, M. (1997). "The effects of expert-generated versus student-generated cognitive organizers on the reading comprehension of students with learning disabilities." *Learning Disabilities Research and Practice, 12* (4), 228–235.

Bromley, K., Irwin-De Vitis, L. & Modlo, M. (1995). *Graphic organizers: Visual strategies for active learning.* New York: Scholastic.

Chall, J. S. (1983). *Stages of reading development.* New York: McGraw Hill.

Chang, K. E., Sung, Y. T. & Chen, I. D. (2002). "The effects of concept mapping to enhance text comprehension and summarization." *Journal of Experimental Education, 71* (1), 5–24.

Dodge, J. (2005). *Differentiation in action.* New York: Scholastic.

Dreher, M. J. (2003). "Motivating struggling readers by tapping the potential of information books." *Reading and Writing Quarterly: Overcoming Learning Difficulties, 19* (1), 25–38.

Duke, N. K. & Bennett-Armistead, V. S. (2003). *Reading & writing informational text in the primary grades: Research-based practices.* New York: Scholastic.

Egan, M. (1999). "Reflections on effective use of graphic organizers." *Journal of Adolescent and Adult Literacy, 42* (8), 641.

Guastello, E. F. (2000). "Concept mapping effects on science-content comprehension of low-achieving inner-city seventh graders." *Remedial and Special Education, 21* (6), 356.

Moore, D. & Readence, J. (1984). "A quantitative and qualitative review of graphic organizer research." *Journal of Educational Research, 78* (1), 11–17.

Pardo, L. S. (2004). "What every teacher needs to know about comprehension." *Reading Teacher, 58* (3), 272–280.

Stead, T. (2006). *Reality checks: Teaching reading comprehension with nonfiction K-5.* Portland, ME: Stenhouse.

Yopp, R. H. & Yopp, H. K. (2000). "Sharing informational text with young children." *Reading Teacher, 53* (5), 410–423.

Management Tip

Model filling in this organizer several times to demonstrate strategies that students might use to complete it independently.

Literature Link

How to Survive in Antarctica by Lucy Jane Bledsoe (Holiday House, 2006).

An engaging memoir filled with photographs, a timeline, fun facts, and survival tips.

Name _____ Alice _____   Date ____ 8/6 ____

Inferences to the Rescue!

Title: ___ Adventure in Antarctica: Happy Camper School ___

Inference

Things you need to know to be happy in Antarctica

page number:
22

How did you infer?

I read the caption under the picture and used prior knowledge.

Meaning

Happy Camper School offers survival training.

Reading Response for Nonfiction: Graphic Organizers & Mini-Lessons © 2008 by Jennifer Jacobson, Scholastic Teaching Resources, page 9

Inferences to the Rescue!

Purpose

Students distinguish between literal and inferential titles and subtitles and extract meaning from those that are inferential.

Introducing the Activity

Tell students that titles and subtitles can help readers determine the intended meaning of a passage. Explain that *literal* meaning says it like it is. *Inferred* meaning requires readers to draw conclusions, relying on surrounding text or prior knowledge to presume the meaning. When a title or subtitle doesn't give enough information, readers might look for clues to its meaning by scanning the book jacket, introductory paragraph, table of contents, and so on, or by recalling what they already know. Then they can make assumptions and inferences.

Using the Graphic Organizer

1. Select a book—such as Lucy Jane Bledsoe's *How to Survive in Antarctica*—that includes a literal subtitle (for example, "What to Pack") and a non-literal subtitle ("The Adventure: Happy Camper School").

2. Say: *The subtitle "Travel to Antarctica: What to Pack" is literal: it makes it clear that the text will tell what to pack for a trip to Antarctica. But the subtitle "The Adventure: Happy Camper School" is less clear. How can I find out what this passage will be about?* Write the non-literal subtitle and its page number on the graphic organizer.

3. Talk about what the subtitle might infer and strategies that can be used to reach that conclusion. Model how to fill in the "Inference" and "How did you infer?" sections.

4. Read aloud a portion of the text under the subtitle. Ask: *Does the inference match the meaning of the subtitle?* Fill in the "Meaning" section.

5. Distribute copies of the organizer for students to use with other texts.

Taking It Further

Challenge students to find books or articles with subtitles. Have them work in groups to classify them as literal or inferred.

Name _____ Date _____

Inferences to the Rescue!

Title: _____

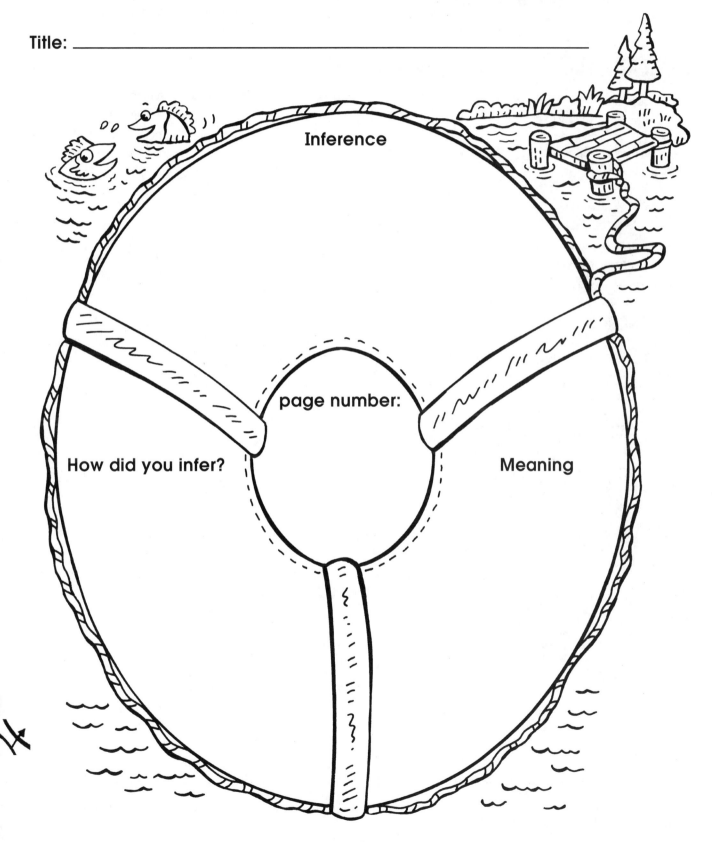

Inference

page number:

How did you infer?

Meaning

Catching the Main Idea

Purpose

Students determine which information is most important and which details are interesting, but less essential, for comprehension.

Introducing the Activity

Ask a volunteer to tell about a recent event, such as something that happened in dance class, at sports practice, or on the playground. Point out that the student likely chose to share the most important information. Ask: *Were other less important details left out?* Help students understand that authors include important details that support the main idea as well as details that may be interesting, but are less important.

Using the Graphic Organizer

1. Choose from an article or book a selection that contains both essential and nonessential facts. Write the title of the selection on the graphic organizer. Then read the passage aloud.

2. Ask: *What is the main idea of the passage? Which details are most important to understanding the main idea?* Record student responses in the appropriate sections of the bucket.

3. Direct students' attention to less important details. Ask: *Which details are fun or interesting, but not necessary to understanding the main idea?* List nonessential details in the puddle.

4. Tell students that when they summarize the main idea of a passage or book, they need only to include the most important details. You might also tell them that when reading for research, it is fine to skim the text to sort the most important information from the nonessential details.

5. Distribute copies of the organizer for students to use with other texts.

Taking It Further

Have students use the information on their organizers to write a summary of their reading selection.

Name ___Ben___ Date ___8/17___

Catching the Main Idea

Title: The Cat With the Yellow Star: Coming of Age in Terezin (chapter 5)

Main Idea:
Performing the opera *Brundibar* gave the prisoners a sense of enjoyment and freedom.

Details that support the main idea:
Nazi officers turned the other way. Everyone in Terezin knew that *Brundibar* represented Hitler when his yellow stars were removed.

Interesting, but less important details:

The plot of the opera

The clothes that Ela wore

Catching the Main Idea

Title: _____

Main Idea:

Details that support the main idea:

Interesting, but less
important details:

Skill

❋ Building Vocabulary

❋ Using Words in Context

❋ Drawing Conclusions

Management Tip

Generate a word list with the class. Then have students complete the organizer independently, choosing words that best help them define the target word.

Literature Link

Delivering Justice: W.W. Law and the Fight for Civil Rights by Jim Haskins (Candlewick Press, 2005).

Relates how a mail carrier helped African Americans register to vote, hold nonviolent protests, and boycott racial discrimination.

Concept Wheel

Purpose

Students learn the meaning of unfamiliar words by linking them to words they already know.

Introducing the Activity

Choose a word from a book or article students have recently read, such as *segregation*, and write it on the board. (Note: Students will find greater success if you explore the meaning of the word after reading the selection rather than before.) Ask students to brainstorm other words that come to mind when they hear the target word. Record all responses to encourage students to feel free to offer associations—even creative ones!

Using the Graphic Organizer

1. After generating a word list with students, distribute copies of the graphic organizer. Have students write the word list on the car window and the target word on the steering wheel.

2. Ask them to choose from the list three words that best help them define the target word. Have them write these words in the other sections of the steering wheel.

3. Invite students to share their word choices with the group or a partner and tell why they chose each word.

4. For additional vocabulary words, distribute copies of the organizer. Have students work individually or in small groups to brainstorm a list of words, fill in the sections of the steering wheel, and then share their responses with classmates.

Taking It Further

Use the organizer to help students define vocabulary words they encounter in science and social studies texts. You might provide three to five unfamiliar words for students to define or assign small groups one word each.

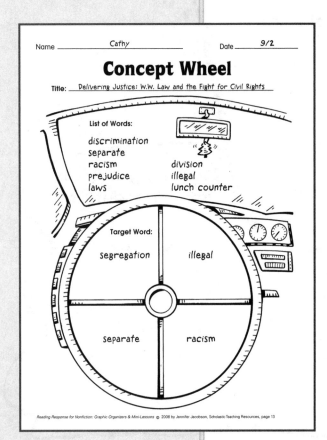

Name _____ Date _____

Concept Wheel

Title: _____

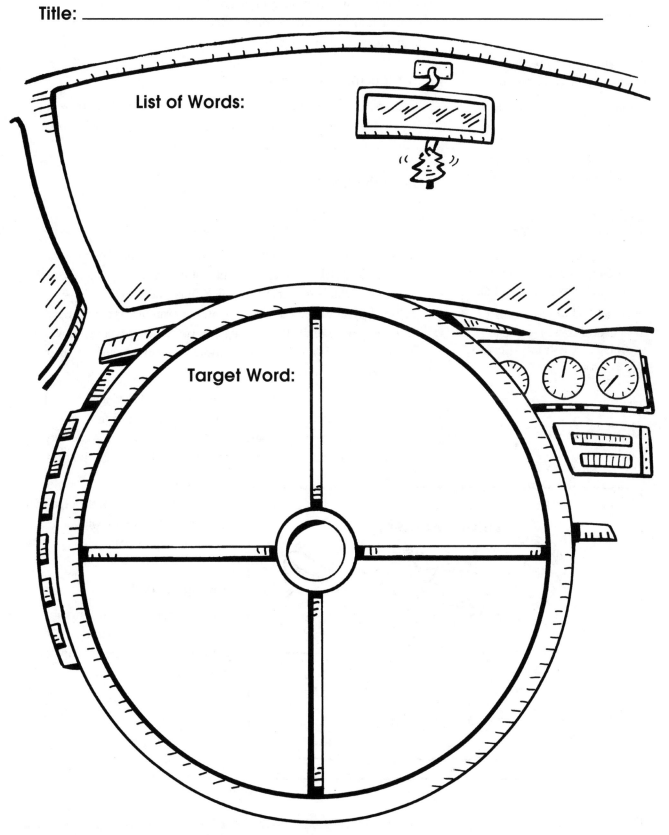

List of Words:

Target Word:

Skill

* Discerning Important Details
* Synthesizing Information
* Recognizing Cause-and-Effect Relationships

Management Tip

Use this organizer on the overhead projector with the whole group. After modeling how to use it, have students complete the organizer independently or in small groups.

Literature Link

Harvesting Hope: The Story of Cesar Chavez by Kathleen Krull (Harcourt Children's Books, 2003).

This picture book biography follows Cesar Chavez from carefree child to powerful advocate for California migrant workers.

Famous Footsteps

Purpose

Students use information from biographies to identify what is most important in a text and determine which life events influenced an individual's accomplishments.

Introducing the Activity

Read aloud a picture book biography or a brief biographical article. Read the entire piece; biographies are often written sequentially and include significant information from beginning to end.

Using the Graphic Organizer

1. Ask students to help you recall the most important details they learned from the text about the subject's life.

2. As students provide details, ask: *Why is that information especially important?* Help them understand that in addition to major accomplishments, facts that show a cause-and-effect relationship are usually considered quite important. For example, as a boy, Cesar Chavez was humiliated as a migrant worker. This experience was one of the reasons he was so motivated to help the plight of migrant workers as an adult.

3. Write any information that students can defend as vital in the appropriate sections on the graphic organizer. Guide them in discerning which information is important and which is ancillary. (Students might require several discussion and practice opportunities to develop this skill.)

4. Distribute copies of the organizer for students to use with other biographical texts.

Taking It Further

Have students use the organizer to organize ideas for writing their autobiographies or the biographies of a classmate.

Name _____Deborah_____   Date ___Sept. 14___

Famous Footsteps

Name of Person: ___Cesar Chavez___

Childhood
A drought forced his family to move from their large ranch in California. He became a migrant worker.

Family
His mother encouraged him not to fight.

Accomplishments
Convinced people to work together.
Preached nonviolence.
Signed first contract in U.S. for farm workers

Education
Cesar had to wear an "I am a clown" sign for speaking Spanish. He graduated in 8th grade.

Interesting Facts
The 1937 drought made the soil rock hard. Many others also had to move away from their farms.

Reading Response for Nonfiction: Graphic Organizers & Mini-Lessons © 2008 by Jennifer Jacobson, Scholastic Teaching Resources, page 15

Famous Footsteps

Name of Person: _____

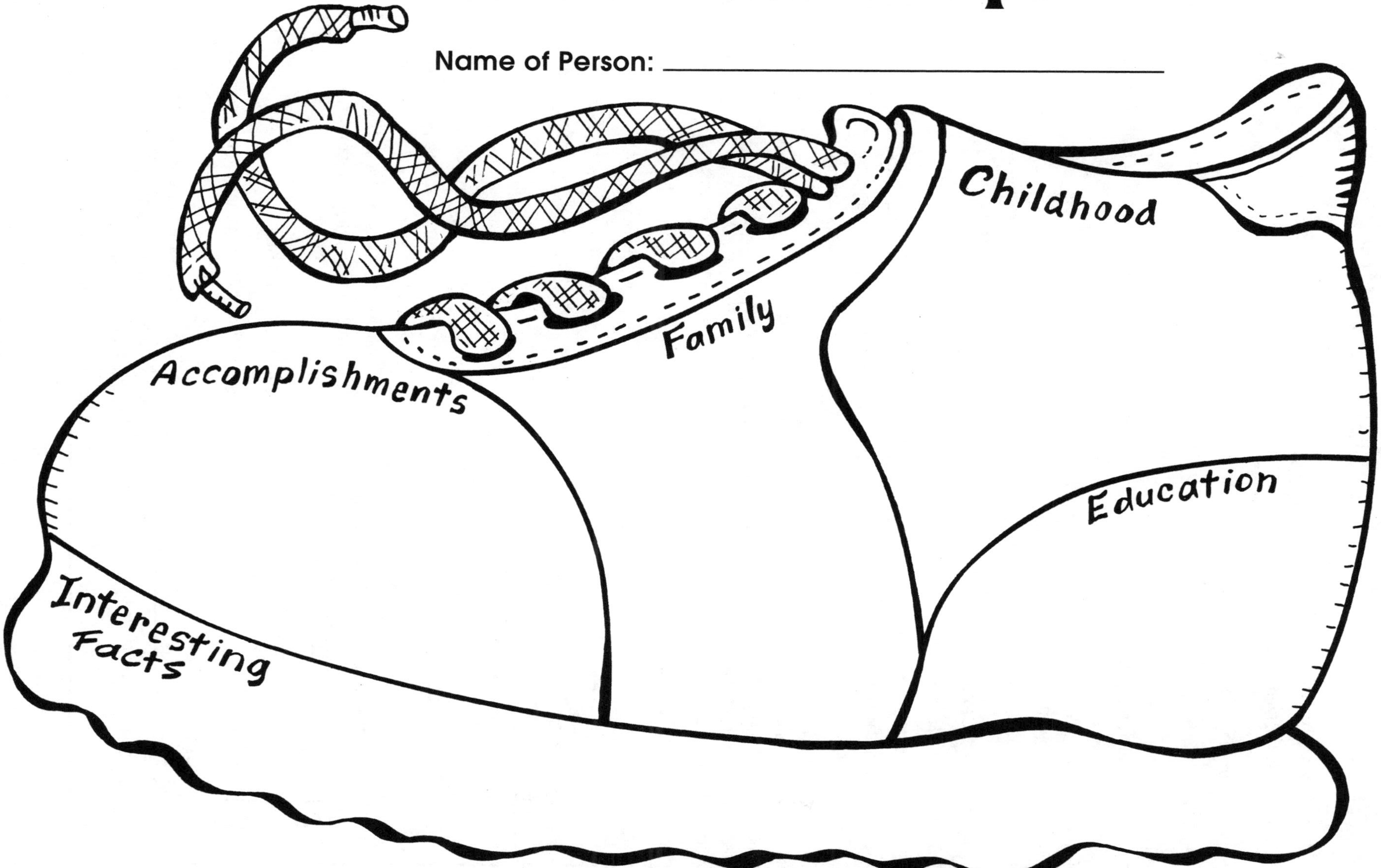

Childhood

Education

Family

Accomplishments

Interesting Facts

In Your Pocket

Purpose

Students focus on nonfiction text features and their importance to reading comprehension.

Introducing the Activity

Show students the pages of a nonfiction text that contains a variety of features including:

* titles
* captions
* sidebars
* subtitles
* charts and tables

* information boxes
* photographs
* maps
* arrows

* graphs
* flow charts
* speech bubbles
* bold print

Tell them that these text features provide extra support for understanding information presented in a nonfiction book or article. Talk about each feature and how it might help readers understand the content and concepts of the passage.

Using the Graphic Organizer

1. Distribute copies of the graphic organizer to individuals or pairs.

2. Have students read a nonfiction selection, paying particular attention to text features.

3. Ask students to write the title on the leaf. Have them list on the chart each type of text feature found in the passage and its page number.

4. After they examine each text feature and its contents, ask students to determine its purpose and fill in the right column, being as specific as possible. For example, for a sidebar text feature, they might write, "lists interesting facts about the person." Have students share their completed organizers with classmates.

Taking It Further

Variety in text features helps enhance understanding for readers of all learning styles. Invite students to tell which text features are most helpful to them and why. For example, some might learn better from viewing maps rather than reading printed directions; others might interpret meaning more deeply from photographs than written detail.

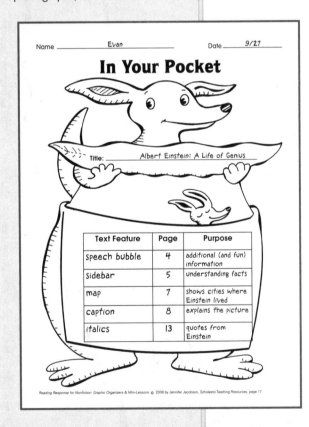

Name ─────────────────────────────── Date ─────────────

In Your Pocket

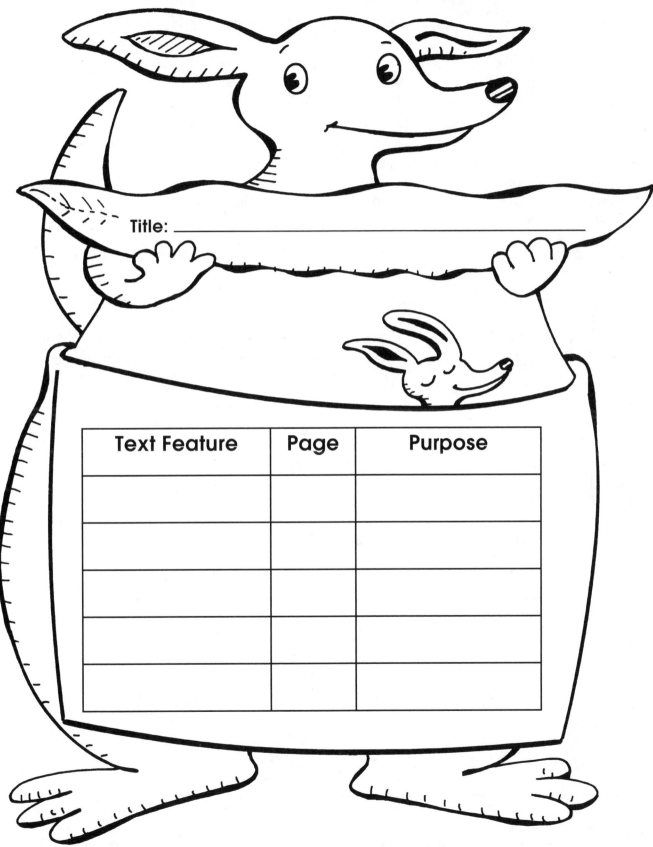

Title: ──

Text Feature	Page	Purpose

* Comparing and Contrasting Genres
* Identifying Text Features
* Making Connections

Literature Link

The Golden Gate Bridge by Craig A. Doherty and Katherine M. Doherty (Blackbirch Press, 1995).

A compelling account of the building of the Golden Gate Bridge, presenting both historic and scientific perspectives.

Pop's Bridge by Eve Bunting (Harcourt, 2006).

Robert and his friend are proud of their fathers, who work on the construction of the Golden Gate Bridge. Includes some factual information.

Nonfiction vs. Fiction

Purpose

Students compare and contrast fiction and nonfiction to develop a greater understanding of both genres, increase their comprehension, and heighten their engagement with the topic.

Introducing the Activity

Choose two picture or easy chapter books on the same topic—one fiction and the other nonfiction. Read the books aloud at separate times to prepare students to use the organizer.

Using the Graphic Organizer

1. After reading both books, distribute copies of the graphic organizer.

2. Have students write the book titles on the appropriate lines on the Venn diagram.

3. Ask students to tell how the contents of the books differ from each other. Guide them to focus on the presence of text features such as maps, graphs, sidebars, and so on in the nonfiction book and the absence of these features in the fiction book. Have them write their responses in the appropriate sections of the diagram.

4. Ask students to tell how the two books are similar. Ask them to record their responses in the overlapping area of the diagram. Explain that although two books might contain the same information, they often present it in very different ways.

5. Have students use the organizer to compare and contrast other nonfiction and fiction book pairs.

Taking It Further

Provide a mixture of fiction and nonfiction books. Ask small groups to page through the books, determine which ones fit each genre, and sort them accordingly. Discuss why each book fits into its particular grouping.

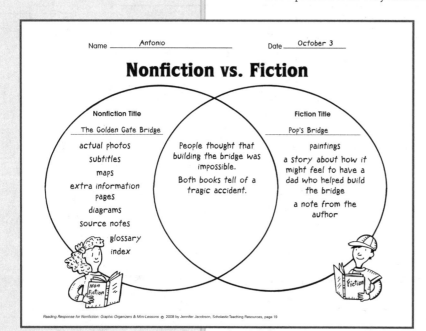

Name _____

Date _____

Nonfiction vs. Fiction

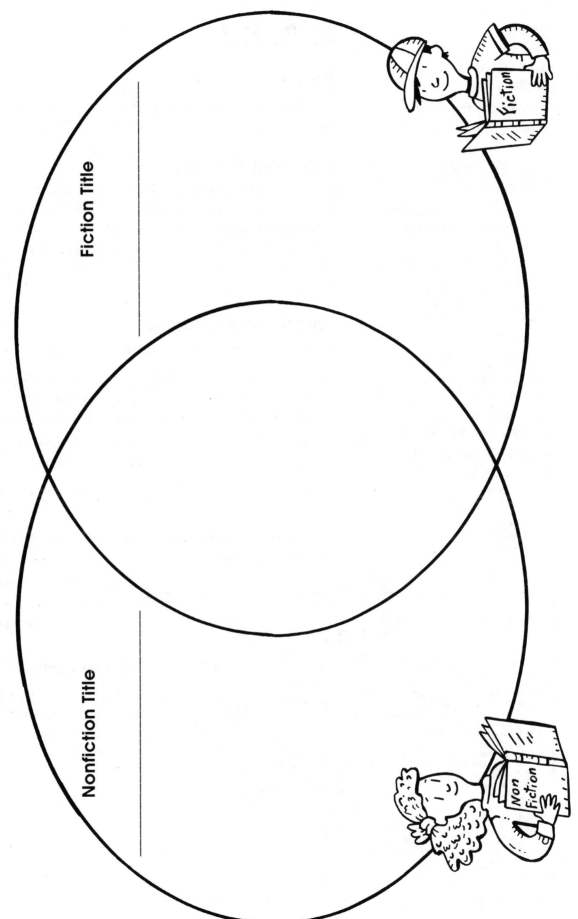

Fiction Title

Nonfiction Title

* Identifying Problems and Solutions

* Summarizing the Main Idea

* Sequencing

Literature Link

"12-Year-Old Makes Students 'Bully Proof'" *WorldNetDaily.com*. April 17, 2004. www.worldnetdaily.com/news/article.asp?ARTICLE_ID=38061

Online article about a boy who prepared seminars and videos to teach his peers how to be "bully-proof."

"Kids in Charge," *Time for Kids: World Report Edition*. May 5, 2006 Vol. 11 (26). www.timeforkids.com/TFK/magazines/printout/0,12479,1189594,00.html

This online article highlights four remarkable kids who started their own businesses.

P. A. R.!

Purpose

Students use the *problem-action-result* organizational pattern of many magazine articles to improve their ability to predict, infer, and summarize.

Introducing the Activity

Tell students that when writing about remarkable people, authors often use an organizational strategy called P. A. R., which means Problem–Action–Result. Ask them to think of articles they've read about individuals who have acted to solve a problem. Ask: *What problem did the person identify? What action did the person take to solve the problem? What was the result?*

Using the Graphic Organizer

1. Provide students with a copy of the graphic organizer.

2. Direct them to read an article that models the P. A. R. organizational pattern—one you have selected from a student magazine or anthology. Have them write the title of the article on the organizer.

3. Ask students to consider the problem the person in the article faced and then write that on the tail section of the rocket.

4. In the middle section of the rocket, have students write the action the person took to solve the problem.

5. Have students write the result of the person's action on the nose section of the rocket.

6. Have students use the organizer with other magazine articles that follow the P. A. R. strategy.

Taking It Further

Students might use the organizer when planning to write a piece about a person who has done something noteworthy.

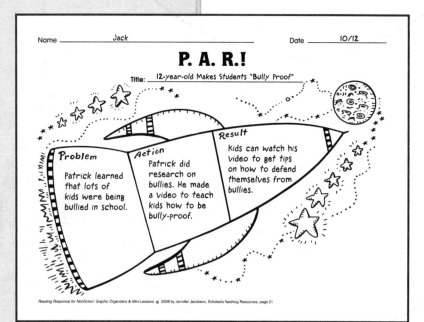

Name _____ Jack _____   Date _____ 10/12 _____

P. A. R.!

Title: 12-year-old Makes Students "Bully Proof"

Problem
Patrick learned that lots of kids were being bullied in school.

Action
Patrick did research on bullies. He made a video to teach kids how to be bully-proof.

Result
Kids can watch his video to get tips on how to defend themselves from bullies.

Reading Response for Nonfiction: Graphic Organizers & Mini-Lessons © 2008 by Jennifer Jacobson, Scholastic Teaching Resources, page 21

Name ———————

Date ———————

P. A. R.!

Title: —————————

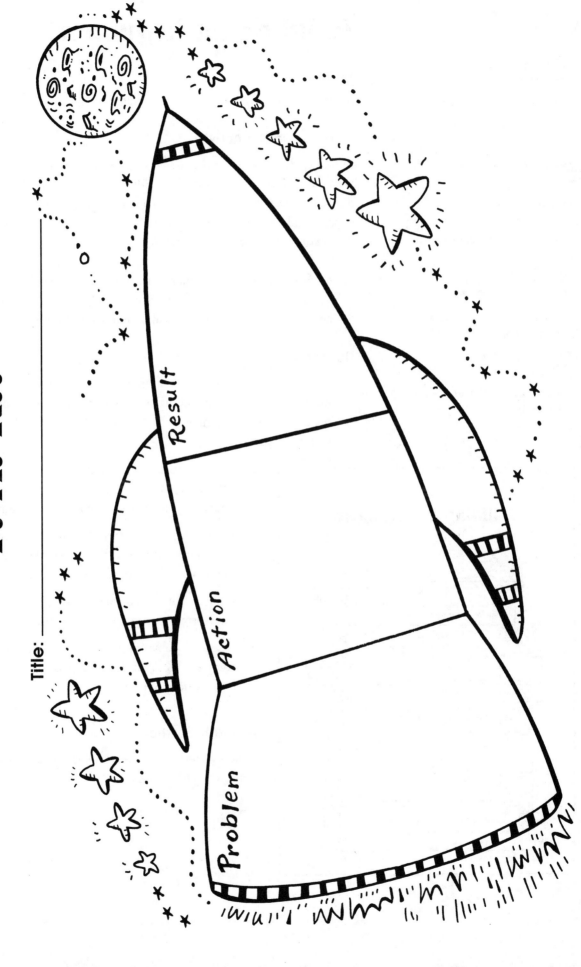

Result

Action

Problem

Skill

* Identifying Persuasive Writing Elements
* Examining Point of View
* Drawing Conclusions

Management Tip

Model how to use this organizer on the overhead projector after reading a persuasive piece with the class.

Literature Link

"Should Public Schools Require Uniforms?" *Junior Scholastic Magazine*. May 11, 1998. 100 (18), 12.

A pro-and-con article in which two students present opposite views.

Building an Argument

Purpose

Students examine the structure of a persuasive essay.

Introducing the Activity

Introduce the topic of the persuasive letter, article, or essay by sharing an example such as "Uniforms Improve Education." Ask: *Why do you think the author wrote this article?* Explain that authors of persuasive pieces seek to share and convince others of their points of view. They usually follow this predictable pattern in their writing:

1. The author presents an opinion in the introductory paragraph.
2. The author states three arguments with supportive details in the body.
3. The author restates his or her opinion in the conclusion.

Using the Graphic Organizer

1. Read aloud the persuasive selection. Stop reading after the introductory paragraph and help students identify the author's opinion. Write the opinion in the "Introduction" box on the graphic organizer.

2. Continue reading the selection. Pause after the author presents the first argument. Write a sentence under "Argument 1" to summarize the point made.

3. Repeat for each argument the author presents. As you do this, talk about specific words the author uses to convince the reader.

4. Read the author's conclusion. Write a sentence to state the author's point of view under "Conclusion."

5. Distribute copies of the organizer for students to complete after independently reading a persuasive letter, article, or essay.

Taking It Further

Invite students to use the organizer to plan for writing their own persuasive essays.

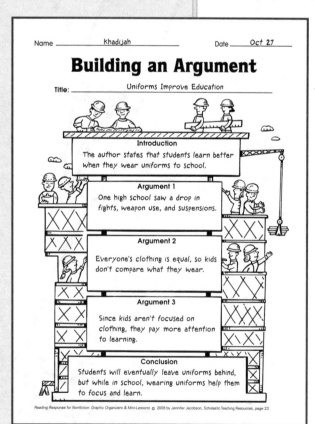

Name _____ khadijah _____ Date _____ Oct 27 _____

Building an Argument

Title: _____ Uniforms Improve Education _____

Introduction
The author states that students learn better when they wear uniforms to school.

Argument 1
One high school saw a drop in fights, weapon use, and suspensions.

Argument 2
Everyone's clothing is equal, so kids don't compare what they wear.

Argument 3
Since kids aren't focused on clothing, they pay more attention to learning.

Conclusion
Students will eventually leave uniforms behind, but while in school, wearing uniforms help them to focus and learn.

Reading Response for Nonfiction: Graphic Organizers & Mini-Lessons © 2008 by Jennifer Jacobson, Scholastic Teaching Resources, page 23

Name _____ Date _____

Building an Argument

Title: _____

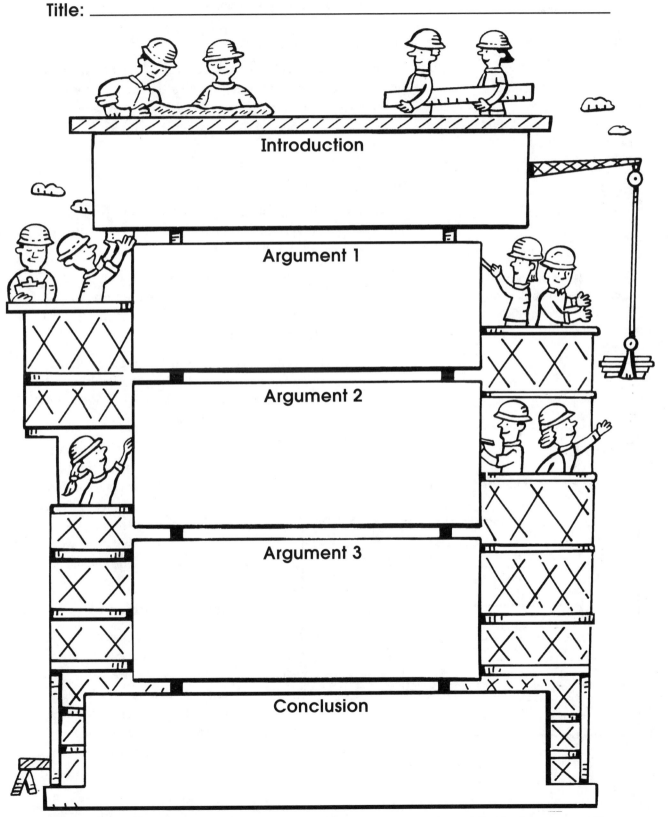

Introduction

Argument 1

Argument 2

Argument 3

Conclusion

Raising Connections

Purpose

Students make text-to-self, text-to-text, and text-to-world connections to increase their reading comprehension.

Introducing the Activity

Read aloud a nonfiction picture book, article, or chapter from a nonfiction book. Tell students that readers understand text more when they connect it to their own personal experiences, other texts that they've read, and even world events. Connections such as these help readers feel a sense of ownership or involvement.

Using the Graphic Organizer

1. Write the title of the reading selection on the graphic organizer. Then share a personal connection that you made when you read the selection. Record your connection on the barn roof.

2. Think of another book, article, or news story that came to mind as you read the selection. Write the name of that text (or a synopsis of it) on the barn. Point out that connecting one text to another is a powerful way to boost understanding.

3. Tell students that nonfiction often gets us thinking about what's happening in the world now or what has happened in the past. Describe a "text-to-world" connection that you made and record that on the silo.

4. Once students understand the function of the organizer, distribute copies to students. Have them complete the organizer on their own, making their own connections to the text you've just read or to another nonfiction text.

Taking It Further

Schedule time regularly for students to read and respond to nonfiction literature to reinforce their understanding and development of the process involved in making text-to-self, text-to-text, and text-to-world connections.

Name _____ Helen _____ Date ____ 11/1 ____

Raising Connections

Title: _____ Moon _____

Text-to-Self
My grandmother told me that some people act crazy during a full moon.

Text-to-World
There isn't life on the moon, but there might be life on Mars.

Text-to-Text
This book reminds me of *Kitten's First Full Moon*. kitten thinks the moon is a bowl of milk and that it's close by.

Name _____   Date _____

Raising Connections

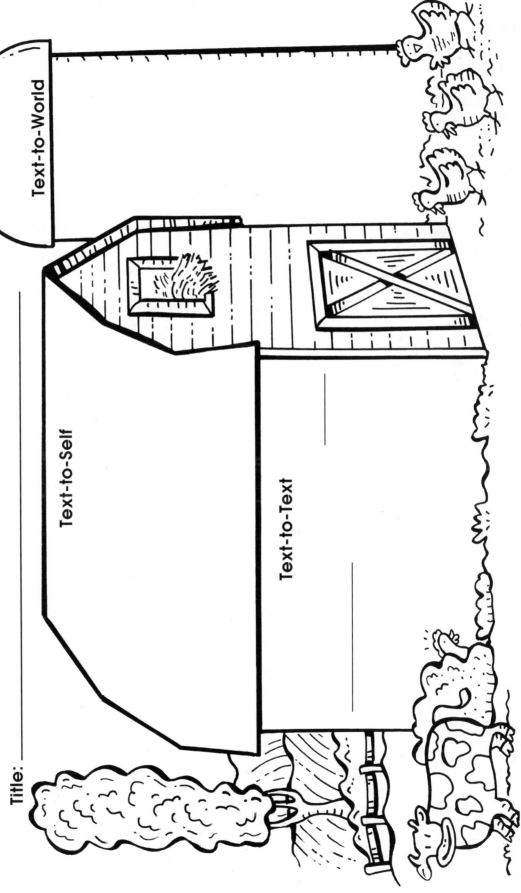

Text-to-World

Title: _____

Text-to-Self

Text-to-Text

Management Tip

After modeling how to use the
organizer, have students complete it
and share their responses during a
literature discussion.

Literature Link

*Flick a Switch: How Electricity Gets
to Your Home* by Barbara Seuling
(Holiday House, 2003).

Describes the discovery of electricity,
how it is generated and distributed,
and early electrically powered
inventions.

Name _____ Ian _____   Date _____ 11/9 _____

Super Inferences!

Title: ___ Flick a Switch: How Electricity Gets to Your Home ___

Facts
Many power plants
use water to turn
the blades of their
turbines.

Inferences

The water must
come from a large
source such as a
river with a dam.

Reading Response for Nonfiction: Graphic Organizers & Mini-Lessons © 2008 by Jennifer Jacobson, Scholastic Teaching Resources, page 27

Super Inferences!

Purpose

Students use facts to make inferences about nonfiction text.

Introducing the Activity

Choose a nonfiction passage to read aloud. Before reading, ask students
to tell what they know about the subject. Remind them that good readers
combine what they already know with what they read in order to fully
understand the text. Good readers also ask questions as they read.

Using the Graphic Organizer

1. Fill in the title of the reading passage on the graphic organizer. Then,
    as you read the passage aloud, pause when you come to a fact that
    raises a question in your mind. For example, in Barbara Seuling's *Flick
    a Switch: How Electricity Gets to Your Home,* you might pause at "Many
    power plants use water to turn the blades of their turbines."

2. Point out the two sides of the cape. Model writing the fact on the
    left side of the cape.

3. As you develop an inference about the fact, voice your thoughts
    and questions out loud. For example, you might say, "I
    wonder where water for the turbines comes from. It takes
    a lot of water to make electricity, so I predict there must
    be a large water source nearby. I see a dam on the river
    in this picture. A dam probably collects enough water for
    the power plant to use."

4. Formulate and write your inference on the right
    side of the cape. Point out that authors count
    on readers to get the full meaning of a text by
    making inferences.

5. Distribute copies of the organizer. Help students
    develop and record their own inferences about facts
    related to the current topic or topics introduced in
    other nonfiction materials.

Taking It Further

Some students might choose facts that do not support
inferences. Help students understand that not all facts
lead to a path of further discovery, and sometimes
authors don't provide enough detail or text features to
make inferences.

Name _____ Date _____

Super Inferences!

Title: _____

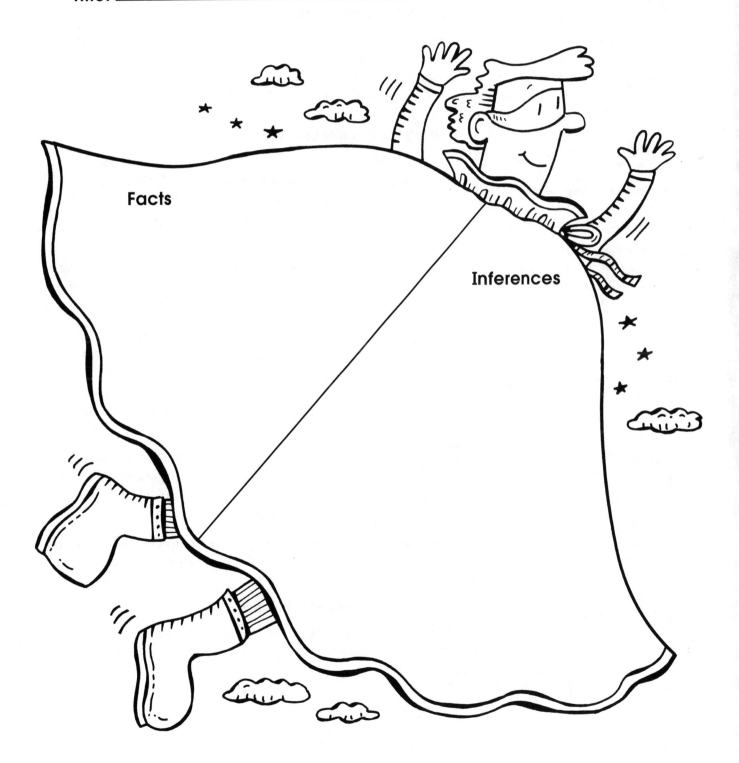

Facts

Inferences

Skill

✴ Examining Author's Purpose

✴ Summarizing Ideas

✴ Making Connections

Management Tip

Invite students to share their responses on the organizer to give them the opportunity to hear a range of reactions and monitor their own reading comprehension.

Literature Link

Ice Bear: In the Steps of the Polar Bear by Nicola Davies (Candlewick Press, 2005).

Lyrical language describes how the polar bear thrives in the Arctic and what the Inuit people have learned from watching *Nanuk*.

Talk With the Author

Purpose

Students employ critical thinking skills as they analyze a text to gain knowledge and study the author's intent.

Introducing the Activity

Talk with students about reasons an author might write about a specific topic. Point out that authors of nonfiction often choose topics that support a cause they believe in, a subject in which they have expertise or a particular interest, or a point they feel needs to be made.

Using the Graphic Organizer

1. Read aloud a nonfiction article or informational picture book such as *Ice Bear: In the Steps of the Polar Bear* by Nicola Davies. Ask a volunteer to summarize the text. Then model how to record the summary in the box at the top of the graphic organizer.

2. Ask: *If you could talk to the author, what would you ask him or her?* Encourage students to generate questions related to the author's writing process, personal experiences with the topic, or reasons for writing the text (such as "Why did you write this book about polar bears?"). Write a student's response in the second box.

3. Ask: *What might the author say if you asked him or her your question?* Write a student's response in the speech bubble on the left (for example, "I wanted to show how amazing it is that the polar bear lives in such a cold climate.").

4. Ask students to share their reactions to what the author might say. Do they agree or disagree? What would they say in return? Write another student's response in the bubble on the right.

5. Distribute copies of the organizer for students to use with other nonfiction selections.

Taking It Further

Encourage students to use the organizer to explore and defend their own purpose in writing nonfiction.

Name _____   Date _____

Talk With the Author

Title: _____

Summary:

If I could talk with the author, I might ask:

The author might say:

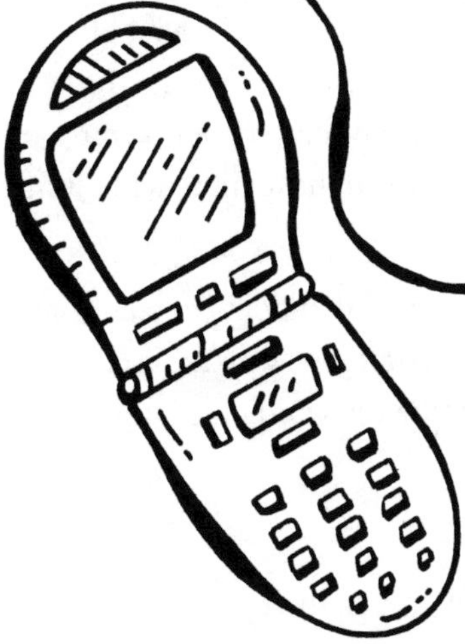

In response, I might say:

❋ Developing Vocabulary-
Building Strategies

❋ Using Context Clues

❋ Examining Word Choice

Management Tip

Introduce this organizer before
students begin reading to heighten
awareness of the strategies they
and others use to decipher
unfamiliar words.

Literature Link

*The Journey That Saved Curious
George* by Louise Bordon
(Houghton Mifflin, 2005).

In 1940, Hans and Margret Rey fled
the German army on bicycles, taking
only a few possessions that included
their manuscripts for children's books.

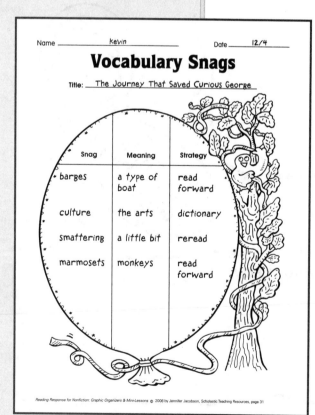

Vocabulary Snags

Purpose

Students identify unfamiliar words and use multiple strategies to define them.

Introducing the Activity

Ask students: *When you're reading, what do you do when you come to a word
you don't know?* List their responses on the board. Some strategies student
might mention include:

❋ using context clues from text or pictures

❋ recalling prior knowledge

❋ consulting dictionaries, glossaries, and other sources

❋ applying analogies

❋ exploring word choice

❋ identifying root words

❋ determining prefixes and suffixes

❋ reading ahead

❋ examining sentence structure

Using the Graphic Organizer

1. Distribute copies of the graphic organizer to students. Have them
   fill in the title of a nonfiction selection, such as Louise Bordon's *The
   Journey That Saved Curious George*. Then, as they read,
   have them record unfamiliar words—or words that snag
   them up—in the left column on the balloon.

2. Encourage students to choose and try several of
   the strategies from the class list to determine the
   meaning of each word. When they come up with a
   suitable meaning for the word, have them write it in
   the middle column.

3. To complete the organizer, ask students to record in
   the right column which strategies were most effective
   in helping them determine the word's meaning.

Taking It Further

Assign each of several small groups three strategies
for determining the meaning of words. Choose the
strategies from the class list or the organizer. Challenge
each group to use only the assigned strategies to try to
unlock the meaning of unfamiliar words they encounter
in a reading selection.

Name _____   Date _____

Vocabulary Snags

Title: _____

Snag	Meaning	Strategy

Skill

❋ Building Knowledge Through Questioning

❋ Tapping Background Knowledge

❋ Locating Information

Management Tip

Encourage attentiveness to the meaning and purpose of text by introducing this organizer before students begin reading.

Literature Link

Earthquakes by Ellen J. Prager (National Geographic Children's Books, 2002).

A clear, step-by-step explanation of how earthquakes occur, including safety tips, vivid illustrations, maps, and an experiment to create an earthquake.

What I Wonder

Purpose

Students explore the strategy of "wondering" about a topic and locating answers to their own questions.

Introducing the Activity

Explain to students that nonfiction text provides readers with information. As a result, it answers many questions—questions that may come up before or during the time readers make their way through the text.

Using the Graphic Organizer

1. Choose a brief nonfiction selection, such as Ellen Prager's *Earthquakes*, to use in modeling how to complete the graphic organizer.

2. Show students the book cover and read the title. Then demonstrate the strategy of recalling what you know and "wondering" about the topic based on information on the cover. For example, by tapping into your own background knowledge, you might say aloud, "I experienced a minor earthquake once. I was in my apartment, and I could hear the dishes rattling in the cupboards."

3. Then wonder aloud about the topic, saying, for example, "Although I've experienced the ground moving during an earthquake, I wonder what *causes* the ground to move." Write your question on the left side of the tent.

4. Read the selection to students, pausing when you reach a part that answers your question. Discuss the findings and write what you learned on the right side of the tent.

5. Distribute copies of the organizer for students to complete using other nonfiction texts.

Taking It Further

Inform students that, often, the text may not provide an answer to a posed question. To help prepare for this possibility, have students list several places that they might go next to find the answer.

Name ___Laura___   Date ___12/14___

What I Wonder

Title: ___Earthquakes___

What I Wonder:

What causes the ground to move during an earthquake?

What I Learned:

When rocks stretch and break, they create an energy that causes the ground to move.

Reading Response for Nonfiction: Graphic Organizers & Mini-Lessons © 2008 by Jennifer Jacobson, Scholastic Teaching Resources, page 33

Name ———————————— Date ————

What I Wonder

Title: ————————————————

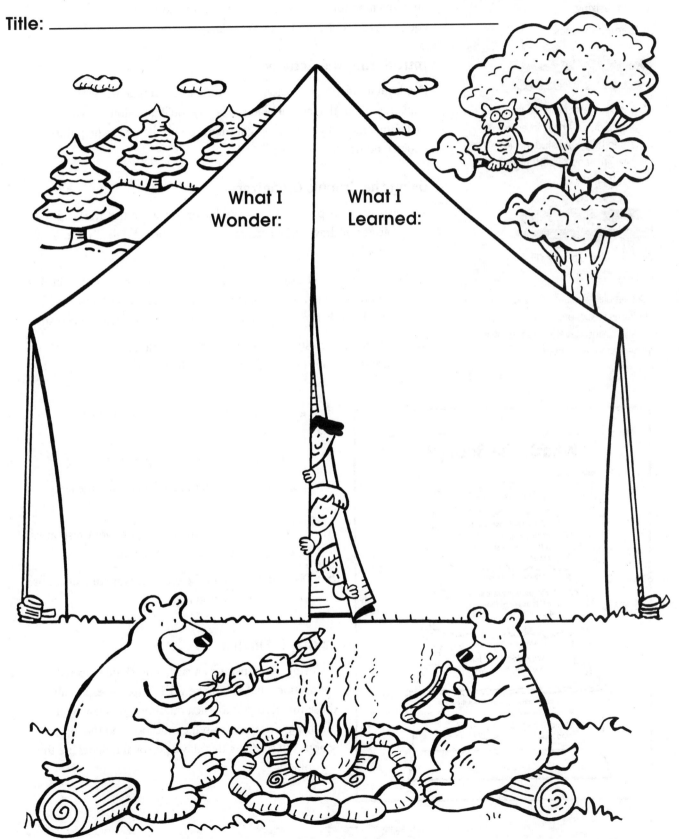

What I
Wonder:

What I
Learned:

* Making Connections Through Questioning

* Synthesizing

* Examining Ideas

Management Tip

After individuals complete this organizer, discuss responses as a class to help lead students to new insights and opportunities for deeper thinking.

Literature Link

Owls by Gail Gibbons (Holiday House, 2005).

Uses labeled illustrations and diagrams to explore the habitats, life styles, and development of owls, as well as environmental hazards that threaten them.

What's the Scoop?

Purpose

Students monitor their own interaction with text to increase comprehension of a nonfiction selection.

Introducing the Activity

Display a nonfiction read-aloud that students are unfamiliar with. Explain to them that as you read the book, you'll talk aloud to yourself to demonstrate how a reader might interact with the text to help improve understanding of what is read.

Using the Graphic Organizer

1. Display a transparency of the graphic organizer on the overhead projector or draw the ice cream dish on the board. Fill in the title of the book.

2. Before reading, tell students the topic of the book and write it on the bottom section of the ice cream dish. Name one fact you already know about that topic. Write the fact on the top section of the dish.

3. Read the book to students, pausing to talk aloud to yourself to demonstrate your own interaction with the text. For example, you might:

   * generate a question that comes to mind as you read.

   * react to information that surprises you.

   * point out something you learned from the text.

4. As you interact with the text, record your responses on the appropriate ice cream scoops.

5. Distribute copies of the organizer for students to use with other nonfiction texts.

Taking It Further

To further demonstrate engagement, share personal connections that you make with the text—especially those that lead you to ask a question. Jot a few words regarding these text-to-self connections on the top scoop. Tell students that these personal touches are the "sprinkles!"

Name _____Luke_____   Date ____1/6____

What's the Scoop?

Title: _____Owls_____

One thing I learned:
There are two types of owls—those with round faces and those with heart-shaped faces.

One thing that surprised me:
Many owls have one ear that is higher than the other.

One question I have:
Why don't we see owls in the wild?

One thing I already know about the topic:
When Barred Owls call, it sounds like they say, "Who? Who cooks for you all?"

Topic
Owls

Name _____ Date _____

What's the Scoop?

Title: _____

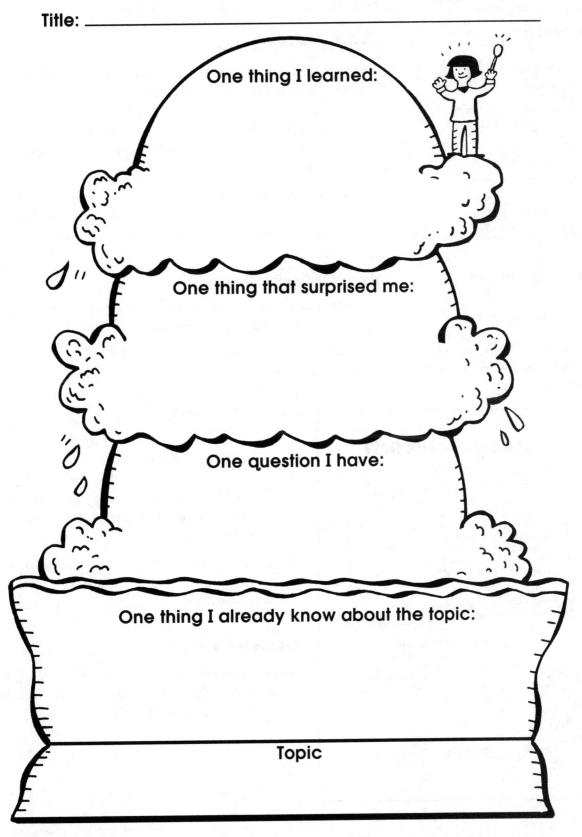

One thing I learned:

One thing that surprised me:

One question I have:

One thing I already know about the topic:

Topic

* Distinguishing Fact From Opinion

* Evaluating Information

* Examining Author's Purpose

Management Tip

Use this organizer on an overhead projector as part of a reading lesson. Later, have students complete the organizer and share their responses during a literature discussion.

Literature Link

"Nebraska Treasure" by Gail Hennessey, *Scholastic News Magazine Online*, June 7, 2006.

An online news story about a fossil-filled park that was once an ancient waterhole. http://teacher.scholastic. com/scholasticnews/news/archive. asp?archive=060806

Which Side of the Net?

Purpose

Students explore ways to differentiate fact from opinion.

Introducing the Activity

Explain that authors of nonfiction often provide both facts and opinions to make a point. To help students distinguish fact from opinion, ask:

* *How do you know when an author has written a fact?* (The author cites a source or backs it up with evidence; readers can look up the fact to confirm it.)

* *How can you tell when an author has stated an opinion?* (The author uses words such as *think, believe, good* or *bad, best, worst, right* or *wrong,* or *should*; an opinion cannot be proven.)

Using the Graphic Organizer

1. Select a short magazine article that contains both facts and opinion. Write the title on the graphic organizer.

2. Begin reading the selection aloud. Ask students to signal when they hear a fact or opinion stated. Ask: *Is that a fact or an opinion?* Discuss student responses. Then write the information on the corresponding side of the tennis court.

3. After completing the organizer, ask: *Why do you think authors include their opinions?* Help students understand that authors usually hope to persuade readers when they present their points of view. (Point out that, ultimately, the reader must determine what he or she believes.)

4. Distribute copies of the organizer for students to use with other nonfiction texts that contain both fact and opinion.

Taking It Further

Have each student write a paragraph containing at least one fact and one opinion. Encourage students to integrate the two in order to persuade readers.

36

Name _____   Date _____

Which Side of the Net?

Title: _____

Facts

Opinions

* Classifying and Categorizing to Build Vocabulary

* Using Context Clues

* Clarifying Word Meanings

Management Tip

Have students complete this organizer in pairs or small groups to pool their knowledge.

Literature Link

Galaxies, Galaxies by Gail Gibbons (Holiday House, 2007).

An explanation of galaxies and how we have come to understand them and their place in the Universe. Illustrations with callouts provide additional facts.

Word Map

Purpose

Students use context clues to determine the meaning of words and increase their understanding and retention by categorizing.

Introducing the Activity

List the following words on the board: *sun, snowflake, raindrop, beach, lotion, umbrella, boots, shovel, bathing suit, raincoat, mittens, hat, coat, scarf,* and *shovel.* As a group, classify the words in different ways: by weather condition (*sun, raindrop, snowflake*), season (*sun, beach, lotion, bathing suit*), function (*bathing suit, raincoat, mittens, hat, coat, scarf*), and so on. Help students note that some words apply to several categories.

Using the Graphic Organizer

1. Preview a magazine or news article, or a nonfiction picture book, to identify at least a dozen words that:

   * may be unfamiliar to students.

   * you want students to retain.

   * will help students link new knowledge to prior knowledge.

2. Write the words on the board.

3. Distribute copies of the graphic organizer. Have students write the title of the selection in the center and the list of words at the bottom.

4. Divide the class into pairs or groups. Instruct students to read the text, watching for words from the list as they read. Afterward, have groups create categories for the words. Ask them to write a category name in each box.

5. Have students group the words according to the categories they created by writing them in the corresponding boxes. Students may wish to add other words from the text to fill out their categories. (This is a great way to enhance their comprehension.)

Taking It Further

Have groups share their organizational patterns and reasoning. The more students hear the same words, the more likely they will remember the word meanings.

Name _____ Juan _____   Date _ Jan. 22 _

Word Map

Category: Galaxy Names	Category: What a galaxy contains
Milky Way Andromeda	gases nucleus gamma rays ultraviolet radiation

Title: Galaxies Galaxies

Category: Astronomers	Category: Equipment
Galileo Newton Hubble	refracting telescope reflecting telescope Hubble telescope

Words:

gases	astronomy	Andromeda	radiation
nucleus	Galileo	Cluster	gamma rays
galaxy	Newton	x-rays	
Milky Way	Hubble	ultraviolet	

Word Map

Category: _____

Category: _____

Title: _____

Category: _____

Category: _____

Words: _____

Skill

* Identifying Problems and Solutions

* Recognizing Cause-and-Effect Relationships

* Examining Text Organization

Literature Link

The Boy Who Drew Birds: A Story of John James Audubon by Jacqueline Davies (Houghton Mifflin, 2004).

This book about Audubon's childhood relates how he created a method for banding birds and solved the mystery of what happened to birds in winter.

A Growing Problem

Purpose

Students identify and explore problem-solving structures within a text.

Introducing the Activity

Explain that when authors decide to present a topic, one of the first questions they try to answer is "How should I organize this information?" Writers must choose an organizational structure that best helps readers understand the material. One frequently used structure is problem-solution. Tell students that in this activity they will explore the problem presented in a nonfiction selection.

Using the Graphic Organizer

1. Write the title of the selection on the graphic organizer.

2. Read aloud the passage. Ask students to identify the problem that the author brings up in the text.

3. Using information from the passage, record on the plant who had the problem, where it occurred, and when the problem existed.

4. Write a summary of the problem on the planter. Then record the solution on the dish under the planter.

5. Distribute copies of the organizer for students to complete independently after reading other nonfiction selections.

Taking It Further

Ask students to brainstorm topics that would lend themselves well to a problem-solution format, such as a crisis (electrical outage), environmental concern (beach erosion), or community issue (housing shortage). Encourage them to use the organizer to explore the problem and possible solutions.

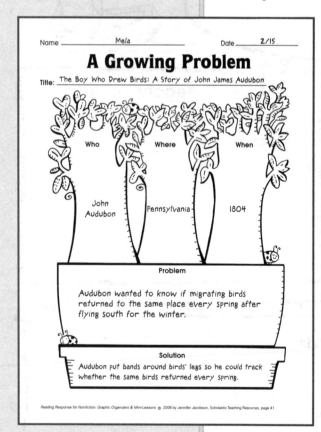

Name _____ Mela _____ Date _2/15_

A Growing Problem

Title: The Boy Who Drew Birds: A Story of John James Audubon

Who — John Audubon

Where — Pennsylvania

When — 1804

Problem

Audubon wanted to know if migrating birds returned to the same place every spring after flying south for the winter.

Solution

Audubon put bands around birds' legs so he could track whether the same birds returned every spring.

Reading Response for Nonfiction: Graphic Organizers & Mini-Lessons © 2008 by Jennifer Jacobson, Scholastic Teaching Resources, page 41

Name _____   Date _____

A Growing Problem

Title: _____

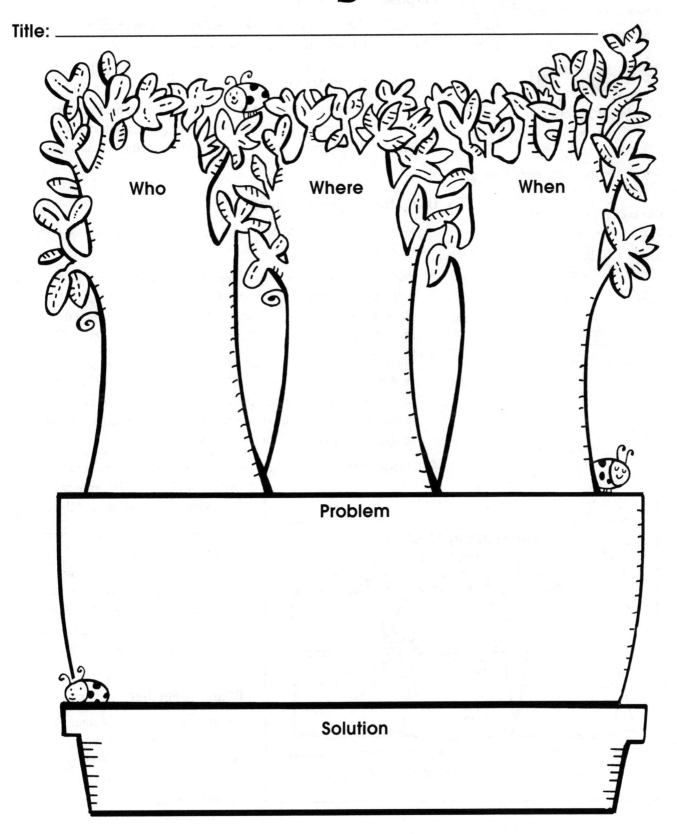

Who   Where   When

Problem

Solution

Reading Response for Nonfiction: Graphic Organizers & Mini-Lessons © 2008 by Jennifer Jacobson, Scholastic Teaching Resources, page 41

* Comparing Sources
* Identifying Text Features
* Skimming Text

Literature Link

The Olympic Summer Games by Caroline Arnold (Franklin Watts, 1991).

Summer Olympics by Clives Gifford (Kingfisher, 2004).

Olympics by Chris Oxlade and David Ballheimer (Alfred A. Knopf, 1999).

Each of these books covers various Olympic-related topics, including history and traditions.

Comparing Design

Purpose

Students build essential research skills as they skim and compare text features of three different nonfiction sources.

Introducing the Activity

Choose three nonfiction books on the same topic. Formulate a question that might be answered by any of the three texts. For example, if using books about the Olympics, you might ask, "Who won the first medal for Tae Kwan Do?"

Using the Graphic Organizer

1. Write your question on the graphic organizer. Record each book title on a shirt.

2. Skim each book with students, pointing out its text features, such as the table of contents, headings, charts, pull-outs, sidebars, glossary, and index. List the features included in each book on the corresponding shirt.

3. Think out loud as you consider which features might lead you to answer the question. For example, you might say, "The index in this book lists four pages on Tae Kwan Do. Maybe the answer is on one of these pages." Explain that skimming can often help readers save time in finding the right book for their purpose.

4. After skimming, ask: *Which book is most likely to answer the question?* Write your choice on the organizer. Then write the reason for your choice.

5. Distribute copies of the organizer for students to complete individually or in pairs. Have students generate a question on a topic of interest and then find library books that they might use to answer their questions.

Taking It Further

Assign a topic to groups of three. Ask each student to bring one nonfiction source on that topic to the group. Have the groups use the books to complete the organizer.

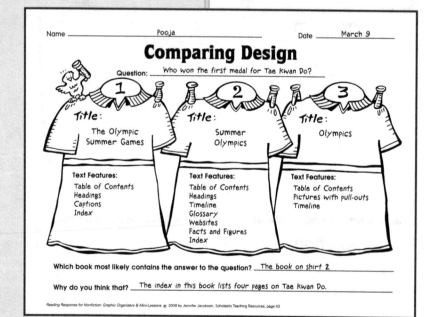

Name _____

Date _____

Comparing Design

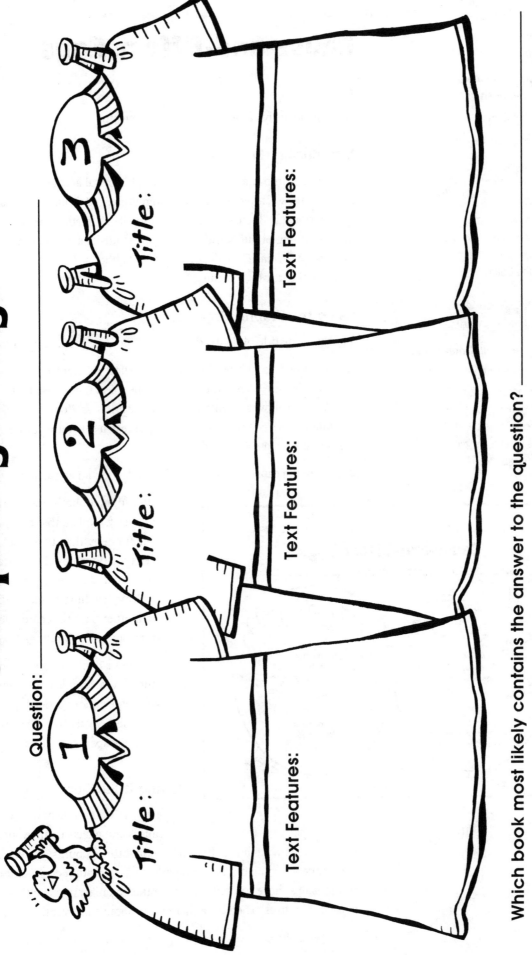

Question: _____

Title: _____ ①

Title: _____ ②

Title: _____ ③

Text Features:

Text Features:

Text Features:

Which book most likely contains the answer to the question? _____

Why do you think that? _____

* Identifying Cause-and-Effect Relationships

* Critical Thinking

* Examining Text Organization

Management Tip

To model how to complete this organizer, copy it onto a transparency or draw hatching chicks on the board.

Literature Link

Ice Cream: The Full Scoop by Gail Gibbons (Holiday House, 2006).

A thorough account of the history of ice cream, how it's made, and other interesting facts. Detailed illustrations label technical or unfamiliar vocabulary.

Cause-and-Effect Eggs

Purpose

Students identify cause-and-effect relationships.

Introducing the Activity

Explain that informational texts such as historical accounts, how-to articles, and scientific matters are often organized around cause-and-effect explanations. By focusing on causes and effects, readers can gain a deeper understanding of our world. Then show students a nonfiction selection, such as *Ice Cream: The Full Scoop* by Gail Gibbons. Tell them that they will examine the text to find cause-and-effect relationships.

Using the Graphic Organizer

1. Write the title of the reading selection on the graphic organizer.

2. Ask students to listen for cause-and-effect relationships as you read the selection. When they identify one, have them raise their hand. Pause to allow students to share their findings. For example, they might observe that when milk is put into a separator (cause), milk and cream are separated (effect).

3. Write the cause on a chick and the effect on an eggshell.

4. After filling in both sides of the organizer, explain that many texts contain more than two cause-and-effect relationships. Tell students they can add to the organizer by drawing hatching chicks on the back or another page to record additional cause-and-effect findings.

5. Distribute copies of the organizer for students to complete independently with other informational texts. Have them share what they learn with small groups.

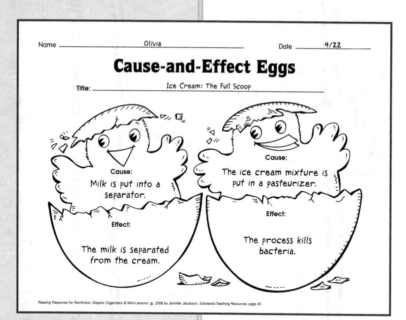

Name _____ Olivia _____   Date ____ 4/22

Cause-and-Effect Eggs

Title: _____ Ice Cream: The Full Scoop _____

Cause:
Milk is put into a separator.

Effect:
The milk is separated from the cream.

Cause:
The ice cream mixture is put in a pasteurizer.

Effect:
The process kills bacteria.

Reading Response for Nonfiction: Graphic Organizers & Mini-Lessons © 2008 by Jennifer Jacobson, Scholastic Teaching Resources, page 45

Taking It Further

Explain that examining and identifying the causes and effects of an event can help students write more thorough, thoughtful accounts. To reinforce their understanding of organizing information around cause-and-effect relationships, have students complete the organizer, focusing on an event in their own lives. Then have them write about that event.

Name

Date

Cause-and-Effect Eggs

Title:

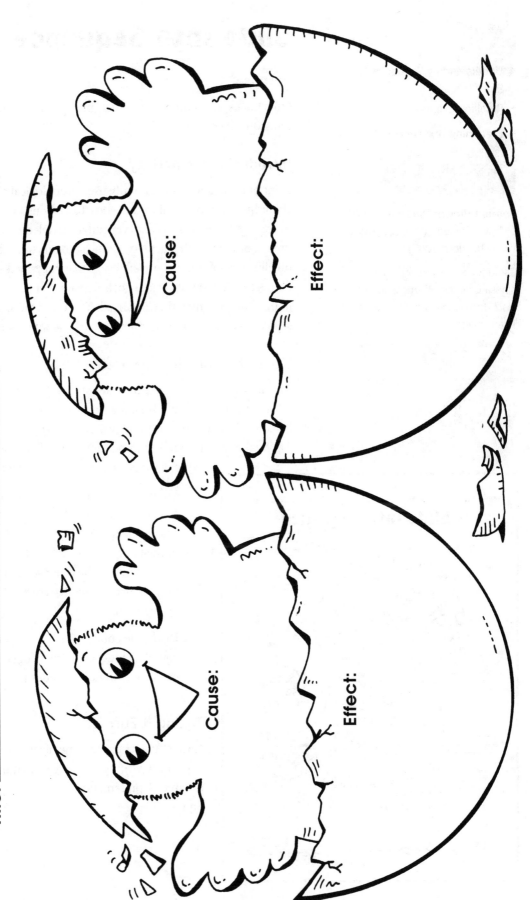

Cause:

Effect:

Cause:

Effect:

Barnum Brown: Dinosaur Hunter by David Sheldon (Walker Books for Young Readers, 2007).

Barnum had a knack for finding dinosaur bones. His most amazing feat? Uncovering and naming the first Tyrannosaurus Rex!

Slide Into Sequence

Purpose

Students explore chronological design in nonfiction texts by identifying the sequence of main events.

Introducing the Activity

Point out that authors commonly use chronological order when writing about historical or significant events. To demonstrate, work with students to create a timeline of recent events that have led to a finished class project or culminating activity. Guide students to understand that the timeline does not include *every* event that happened—just the major events that led to the desired goal. Explain that the events are presented in the *order* in which they occurred. Then read aloud a nonfiction text, such as David Sheldon's *Barnum Brown: Dinosaur Hunter*.

Using the Graphic Organizer

1. After reading the selection, have students work together to determine the main events and the order in which they happened. Remind them that although the author may include many events leading to the final one, some are less important than others. Help them determine which events are the most important.

2. Fill in the title of the selection on the graphic organizer. Then model how to complete the organizer. To do this, record the first main event in the top section of the slide. Write additional main events in the other sections in the order that they occurred. Finally, write the last main event on the pool.

3. Distribute copies of the organizer for students to complete independently using other nonfiction texts based on chronological design.

Taking It Further

Have students use the organizer to plan their own expository writing. Or suggest that they use it to prepare for an oral presentation by recording their major points on the slide.

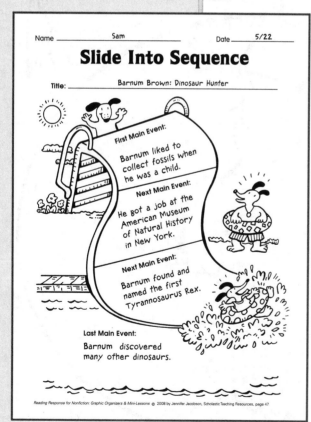

Name _____   Date _____

Slide Into Sequence

Title: _____

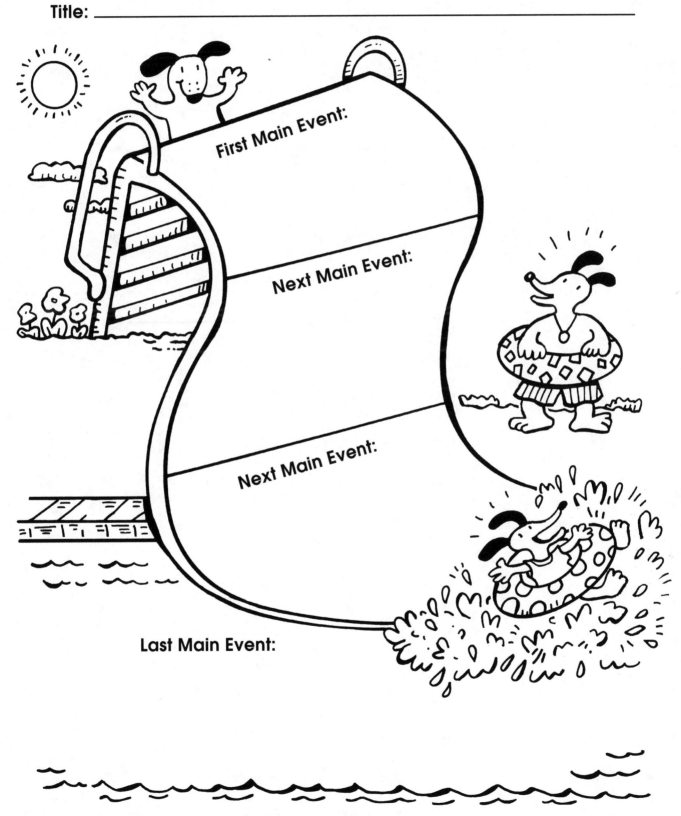

First Main Event:

Next Main Event:

Next Main Event:

Last Main Event:

Notes: